How to trade stock or commodities or cryto currency or index using simple strategy

1. What is Intraday trading.

- Margin buy
- Margin sell

2. Main elements of trading

    a. Candle - bullish, bearish and indecision candle

    b. Edge & Risk mgt

    C. Money mgt

    d. Psychology

3.. List of strategy to find out edge.

- Gap up strategy.
- Gap down strategy.

4. Trade plan.

What is intraday trading:-

Margin Buy

1. Directly buy from NSE Market, 5-time leverage will be provided by stockbroker.
2. Sell directly in NSE market

Example of margin buy

Icici bank I expect can go up from 600 to 615, with stop loss as 590

1. Entry price is at 600 for 1 qty
2. Profit target is 615
3. 3. Stop loss at 590

Margin sell

1. Leverage and stock will be provided by broker
2. You can sell the stock in NSE market
3. One stock goes down you can buy from NSE market
4. Broker will take back the stock from you

Trader am going to sell--- broker -- share desposity -- trade sell share in market.
before end of the day -- he will buy from market --- broker-- share depository.

Example of margin Sell

Icici bank I expect can go down from 600 to 580, with stop loss as 610.
1. Entry price is at 600 for qty 1
2. Profit target is 580
3. Stop loss at 610

How to identify Bullish or bearish candle

Bullish candle

Check list for bullish candle

1   Close and high of present candle should be more than previous candle close and high

2   =open-close/high-low X100 should be more than 50%

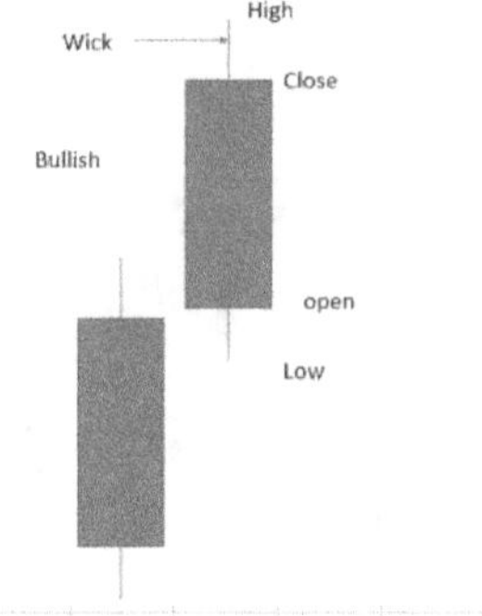

High- low   17.9

Open-close   17.15   Body of candle

Bullish candle 95.81005587   =open-close/high-low X100   More than 50%

Bearish candle

Check list for bearish candle

1. Close and high of present candle should be less than previous candle close and high.
2. '=open-close/high-low X100 should be more than 50%.

Bearish candle

high   24.8

low   12.85

open   24.7

close   14.7

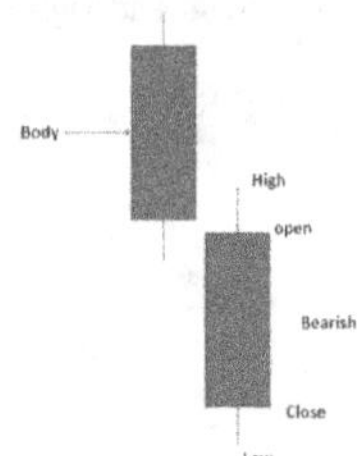

High- low   11.95

Open-close   10   Body of candle

Bearish candle83.68200837   =open-close/high-low X100   More than 50%

High- low   11.95

Body of candle   Open-close   10   83.7

In Decision candle

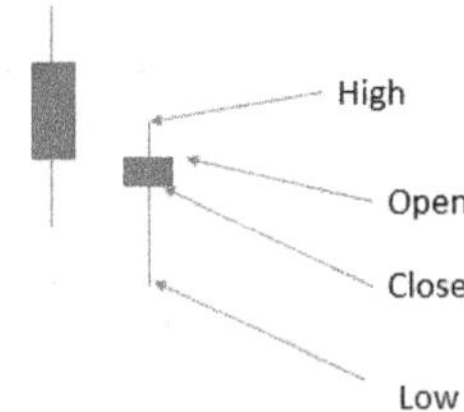

Check list for Indecision candle

1. =open-close/high-low X100   :- should be less than 50%

Element of trading :- Edge, Risk and Money management

What is Edge :- what is the probability of success for my strategy

Example :-

Let assume:- probability of success for my strategy = 50%

Risk: rewards :- 2:5

Assume am buying only 1 quantity

ICICI bank	100	105
Entry	buy	100
SL exit	SL	98
Profit target	Profit target	105
Risk	Entry - SL	100-98 = 2
Reward	Profit target - Entry	105-100=5

After 10 trade my result :-

Trade	Success	loss	Total profit
1	1	0	5
2	0	1	-2
3	0	1	-2
4	1	0	5
5	0	1	-2
6	1	0	5
7	0	1	-2
8	0	1	-2
9	1	0	5
10	1	0	5
Overall	5	5	15

Explanation in details :-

What is
Edge ?   Probability of success & Risk/ reward will be given by my strategy

Risk and Money Mgt

			Capital Risk	Capital reward
			250	500
Capital	Risk per Trade in %	Propability of success %	Risk	Reward
2500	10	50	1	2

Scenario :-
1   **Sequence is success and Loss comes next to next**

Trade		Trade result	Profit/Loss	Principle left
	1	Loss	-250	2250
	2	Success	450	2700
	3	Loss	-250	2450
	4	Success	490	2940
	5	Loss	-250	2690
	6	Success	538	3228
	7	Loss	-250	2978
	8	Success	595.6	3573.6
	9	Loss	-250	3323.6
	10	Success	664.72	3988.32

Scenario :- 2   **Sequence is 1st 2 loss, 2nd 2 success sequence**

Trade		Trade result	Profit/Loss	Principle left
	1	Loss	-250	2250
	2	Loss	-250	2000
	3	Success	400	2400
	4	Success	480	2880
	5	Loss	-250	2630
	6	Loss	-250	2380
	7	Success	476	2856
	8	Success	571.2	3427.2
	9	Loss	-250	3177.2
	10	Loss	-250	2927.2

Scenario :-
3   **Sequence is 1st 3 loss, 2nd 3 success sequence**

Trade	Trade result	Profit/Loss	Principle left
1	Loss	-250	2250
2	Loss	-250	2000
3	Loss	-250	1750
4	Success	350	2100
5	Success	420	2520
6	Success	504	3024
7	Loss	-250	2774
8	Success	554.8	3328.8
9	Success	665.76	3994.56
10	Loss	-250	3744.56

Scenario :-
4   **Sequence is 1st 2 loss, 2nd 2 success sequence**

Trade	Trade result	Profit/Loss	Principle left
1	Loss	-250	2250
2	Loss	-250	2000
3	Loss	-250	1750
4	Loss	-250	1500
5	Loss	-250	1250
6	Success	250	1500
7	Success	300	1800
8	Success	360	2160
9	Success	432	2592
10	Success	518.4	3110.4

How to calculate Qty for a trade

ICICI bank expect to go down from 420 to 400, with SL 430

	Risk Amount	**250**
ICICI	Entry	420
	Profit Target	400
	SL	430

Risk = (SL – Entry) = 430 – 420 = 10
Rewards = (entry – Profit target) = 420-400 = 20

	Risk: Reward	10	20
		1	2

Qty to buy	25	(calculation details =Risk amount/(entry price- SL)

<u>**Psychology of trading:-**</u>

Your decision based on

1. If you lose money, you will take irrational decision

2. you will take more than prescribed risk

3. whenever you are feeling Greed or fear

you will loss self control if you watch the screen/ chart more than 1 hours

you should not have preconceived notion in your mind

eg:-

1. I entered the trade, as per my strategy it will give 1:2 risk reward. But it did not give.

2. I should not have thought of any news from outside environment.

Learn from Failure :- we should keep record of trading both mechanical as well as emotional level you should record you trade daily and check what is working not working

     1   AS per my startegy it touched SL and went up. - lesson learnt check your strtegy for correction of SL.

     2   I have traded more than 1 trade, to get back my proift which result in multiple trade and lost more than 20%

Mental Rehearsal

1.I will do one trade per day

2. I will mentally rehearse my startegy, atleast 10 time in morning, after noon and before go to bed.

3.I will risk only 3 % per trade in Margin trading.

Trade Log example:-

Date	Mechanical	Emotional	No of trade	Succe ss	Not succe ss	Prof it
3-Sep-20		Urge to earn money immedetely because of news of Job loss by Soodi	40	10	30	No
11-Sep-20		Initial trade in loss, want to regain the loss, lead to over trade - Loss aversion	12	2	10	No
14-Sep-20	Falling from Daily and 4 HR SZ, went till the loss of Initial SZ low but came out in middle of down trend	Missing out of profit so went again	8	4	4	Yes

Strategy details :-

How to find out Gap up or Gap down

https://www.nseindia.com/market-data/pre-open-market-cm-and-emerge-market

Go to above site and find out Gap up or down, atleast .75 to 1%

https://chartink.com/stocks/icicibank.html

Strategy 1:- GAP UP

Find below in 5 or 10 or 15 min chart

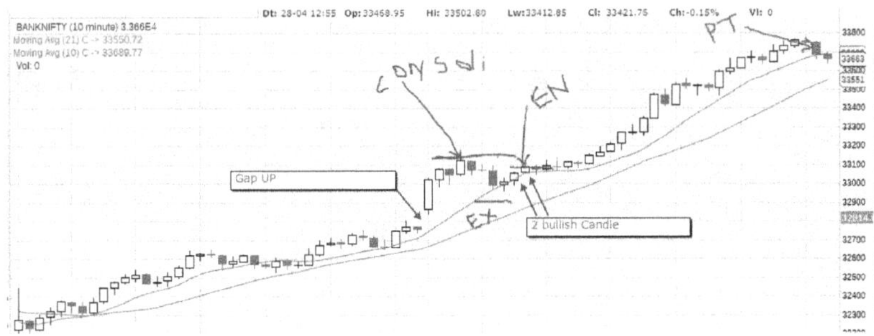

Point to consider:-

1   Gap up + 1st 15 candle break out should happen

2   Consolidation for at least 1 to 1.5 Hours change the candle stick time frame from 5min to 20 min

3   In decision candle and bullish candle formed inside the consolidation

4   Entry above bullish Candle EN or support formed in gap range

5   SL .5 % of Indecision candle low or any candle low at consolidation. EX (32785)

6   Profit target whenever Bearish candle break previous Bullish candle.

7   entry and stop loss should not be more than 1.5% of stock price

Strategy 2 :- GAP Down

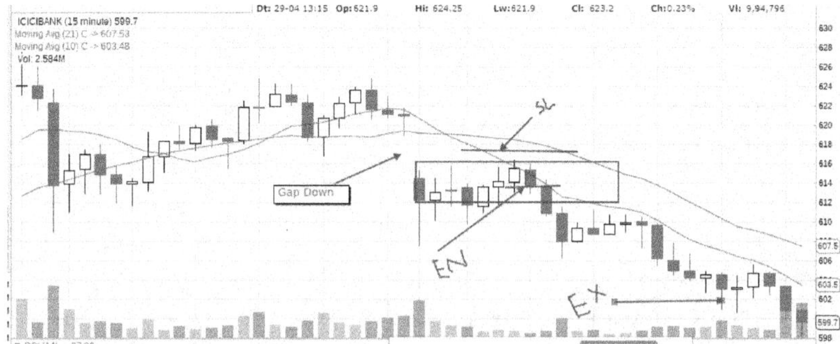

Point to consider

1 Gap Down and 1st 15 min candle should break.

2 Consolidation for at least 1 to 1.5 Hours change the candle stick time frame from 5min to 20 min

3 In decision candle and Bearish candle formed inside the consolidation

4 Entry below Bearish Candle EN or Resistance formed in the Gap

5 SL .5 % of Indecision candle high . EX (620) any candle High at consolidation

6 Profit target whenever Bullish candle break previous Bearish candle.

Trade Plan example: -

1) Cover Sheet:

   1. Trading, to meet my financial needs.

2) Purpose of Trading:

   1. To make my family financial abundance.

   2. For my daughter's higher education in future.

   3. To donate 20% to needy person.

3) Trading Style:

   1. My trading style is Margin Trading in Nifty 100 stocks.

   2. I need to focus only on Intraday trading chart of Nifty 100 stocks and become expert on margin trading.

4) Goal:

1. I will follow the rules of intraday trading what I defined consistently.

2. I will go through chart daily for 1 hour to find out strategy after mkt hour

3. Psychology related book I will read for Mind control.

5) Market want to trade:

I want to margin trade in nifty 100 stocks from 9.15 am to 3.30pm. I need to be expert on margin trading in Nifty 100 stocks.

6) Effective routine:

1) Beginning of trade. 8.15 to 9.15 meditation to keep my mind calm and emotional level also calm. I will read plan morning, afternoon and evening.

2) Checking news, checking the pre market indices (9 to 9:15) and check for my strategy and the chart of nifty 100 stocks.

3) 9.15 to 3.30 pm checking for high probability trade by monitoring 5min per 30 minutes, after 3.15, record the trade both mechanical and internal data(emotional level).

7) I will take my risk on each trade by trading one trade. I will risk only two percent of my capital on any trade. My daily stop loss will be 2 % of capital once my stop loss reach, I will stop my trade and come out from stock market monitoring. I will trade only risk reward is more than 1:1.5

8) Protocols:

I will follow any one of the five strategy and check for the chart in 1hr 30 mins 15 mins 10 mins or 5 mins.

I will sell only gap down, bearish, bearish indecision bearish.

I will buy only gap up, bullish, bullish, indecision, bullish.

Common focus the now moment and follow the process irrespective of result.

Selection of Stocks:

a) Go to fatafat stock screener.

b) Open the excel sheet

c) In K column, sort from Z-A.

d) Look for the stocks which shows More than 1% in K column and in L column nothing should be there and also consider the column S and T which has Above R1 and R2. Select those stocks and and look for chart of those particular selected stocks for Buying strategy. These points for Gap up.

1) Again In K column, sort from A-z.

2) Look for the stocks which shows More than -1% in K column and in L column nothing should be there and also consider the column P and Q which has Support S1 and S2. Select those stocks and look for chart of those particular selected stocks for Selling Strategy. These points for Gap down.

We can consider the stocks which has Runaway.

Gap up:

a) Consolidation for atleast 1to 1.5 hours, change the candle stick time frame from 5min to 20 min

b) Indecision candle and bullish candle formed inside the consolidation

c) Entry above Bullish candle EN

d) SL .5% of indecision candle low or any candle low at consolidation

e) Profit Target whenever the bearish candle breaks the previous bullish candle.

f) Entry and Stop loss should not be more than 1.5% of stock price.

Gap down:

a) Consolidation for atleast 1to 1.5 hours, change the candle stick time frame from 5min to 20 min

b) Indecision candle and bearish candle formed inside the consolidation

c) Entry below Bearish candle EN

d) SL .5% of indecision candle high or any candle high at consolidation.

e) Profit Target whenever the bullish candle breaks the previous bearish candle.

f) Entry and Stop loss should not be more than 1.5% of stock price.

You can visit below youtube channel for explanation :- s

https://www.youtube.com/channel/UC0LiPUHdscecyu5dbcSX6qg